TREASURY OF LITERATURE

TAKE-HOME BOOKS

SIDEWALKS SING

HARCOURT BRACE & COMPANY
Orlando Atlanta Austin Boston San Francisco Chicago Dallas New York
Toronto London

Copyright © by Harcourt Brace & Company

All rights reserved. No part of this publication may be reproduced or transmitted in any form or by any means, electronic or mechanical, including photocopy, recording, or any information storage and retrieval system, without permission in writing from the publisher.

Permission is hereby granted to reproduce the Copying Masters in this publication in complete pages for instructional use and not for resale by any teacher using TREASURY OF LITERATURE.

Printed in the United States of America

ISBN 0-15-303599-4

1 2 3 4 5 6 7 8 9 10   082   97 96 95 94

CONTENTS

SIDEWALKS SING

Afraid of Everything (Ronald Morgan Goes to Bat)

A Voice in the Trees (Matthew and Tilly)

Nothing to Do (Arthur's Pet Business)

Best Friends (I Have a Sister—My Sister Is Deaf)

Perfect Stew (The Wolf's Chicken Stew)

The Secret Friend (Everett Anderson's Friend)

The Gigantic Package (Mitchell Is Moving)

It's Not Fair! (Jamaica Tag-Along)

Mallard's Adventure (Abuela)

The Twin Detectives (Six-Dinner Sid)

Disgrace in Dog Town (Old Henry)

Robot Camp (Little Penguin's Tale)

New Friends Festival (Fiesta!)

Favorite Things (Miss Eva and the Red Balloon)

Harcourt Brace School Publishers

TAKE-HOME BOOK
SIDEWALKS SING
Use with "Ronald Morgan Goes to Bat."

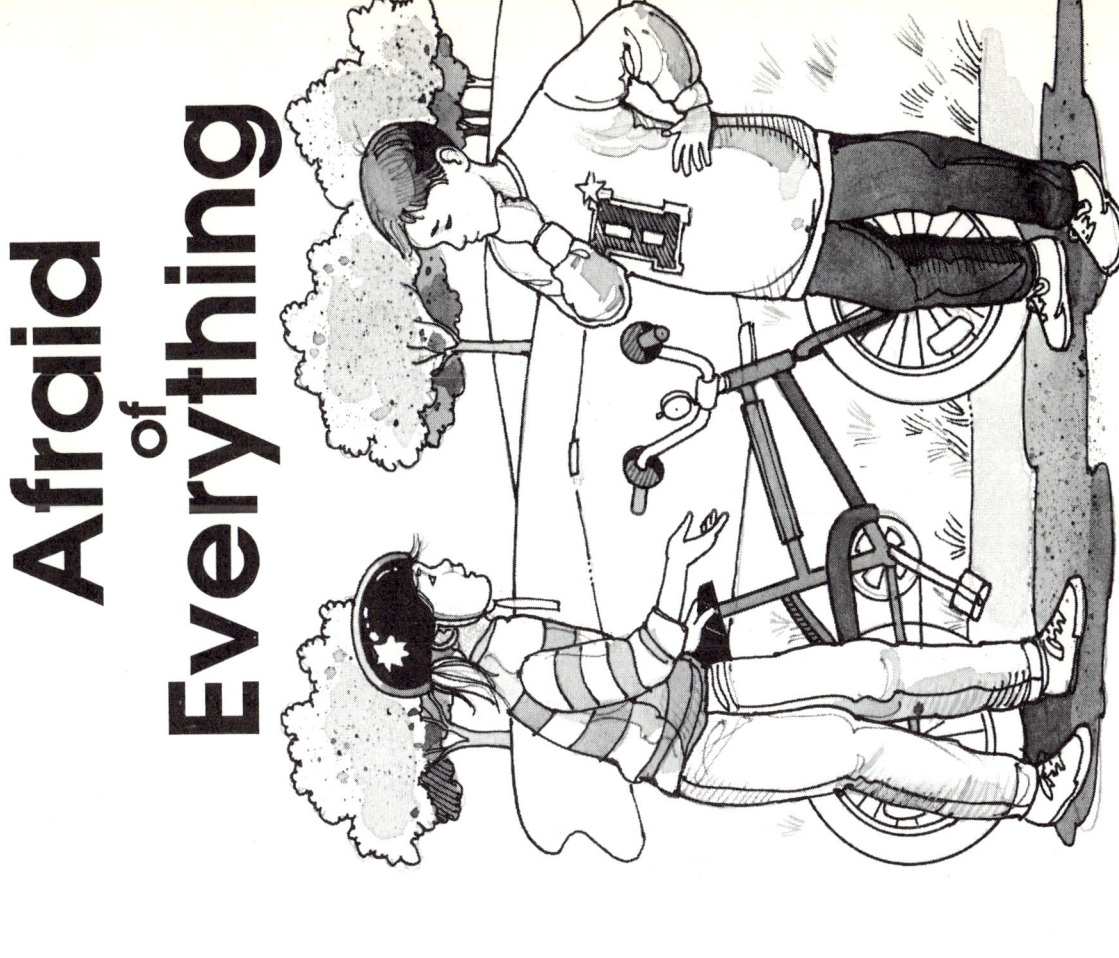

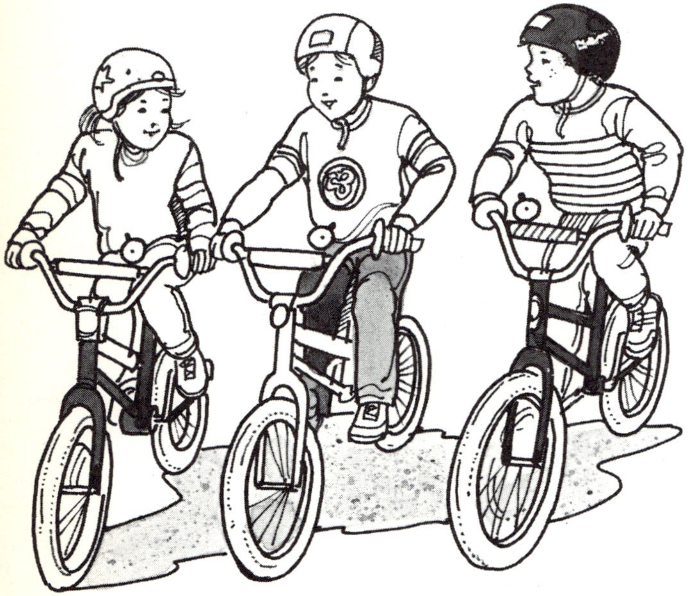

HARCOURT BRACE & COMPANY

Afraid of Everything

by Ellen Keller

Sammy didn't know much about riding bikes. He didn't have a bike of his own. Ann wanted Sammy to practice riding *her* bike.

"You just need to practice," Ann said. "You can have the first turn."

"It's your bike," said Sammy. "You take the first turn."

A few days later, Sammy was out on the field. He had a new bike. A boy came over.

"Hi, my name is David," said the boy. "I know that you're Sammy. I heard that you help kids learn to ride bikes. Will you help me?"

Sammy smiled at the boy. "I will help you," he said. "You don't have to be afraid. You can do it if you practice."

And that's just what Sammy and his new friend did!

That night Sammy's mother heard the whole story. "I knew you could do it," she said. "I was afraid when I rode my first bike. But then I got over it."

"Me, too," said Dad.

"Me, too," said Sammy.

When Sammy closed his eyes, he felt so proud of himself. Now no one could say he was afraid of everything ever again.

So Ann got on her bike and rode down the bike path. Sammy saw Ann race across the field and then turn to come back.

Ann called to Sammy. "Next it will be your turn," she said. "You can get on my bike and go across the field. You'll like it. You'll see!"

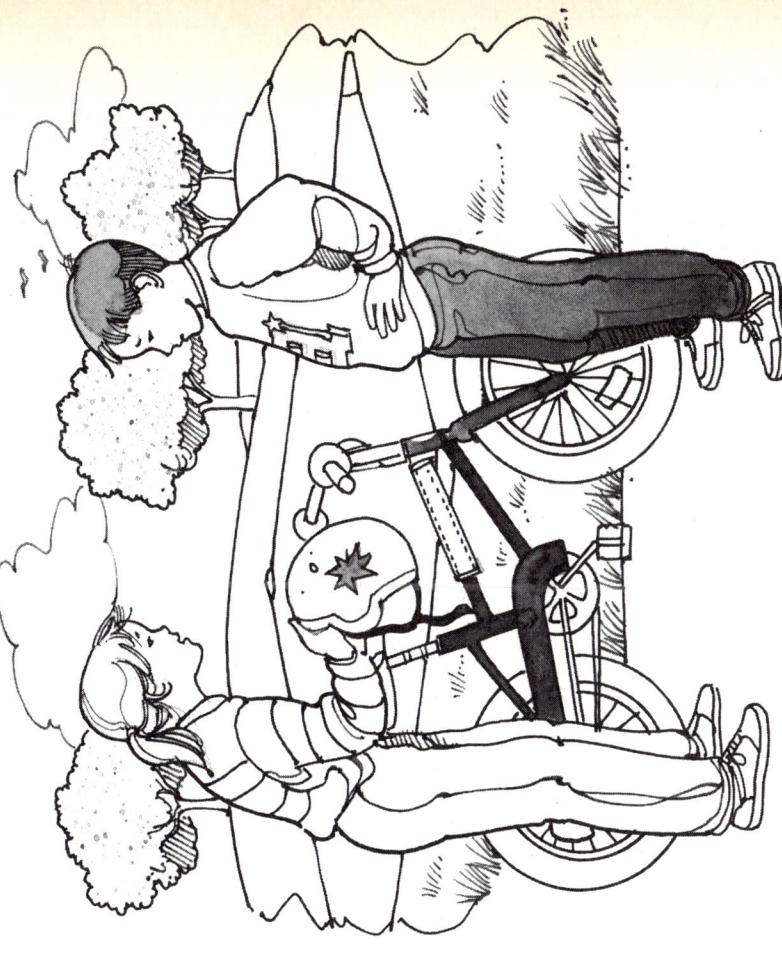

Sammy rode and rode. Then Sammy said, "You can let go, Dad. I'm not afraid anymore!" Sammy rode the bike all the way around the field.

Ann came running out of her house. "I knew you could do it, Sammy!" she yelled.

"It's your turn to ride your bike now," said Sammy. "Thanks for letting me use it. I'm going to get my own bike. Then I can practice every day."

"Why don't you take a turn again?" asked Sammy. "I can practice after you."

"I don't need practice," said Ann. "But *you* do. Are you afraid to get on the bike?"

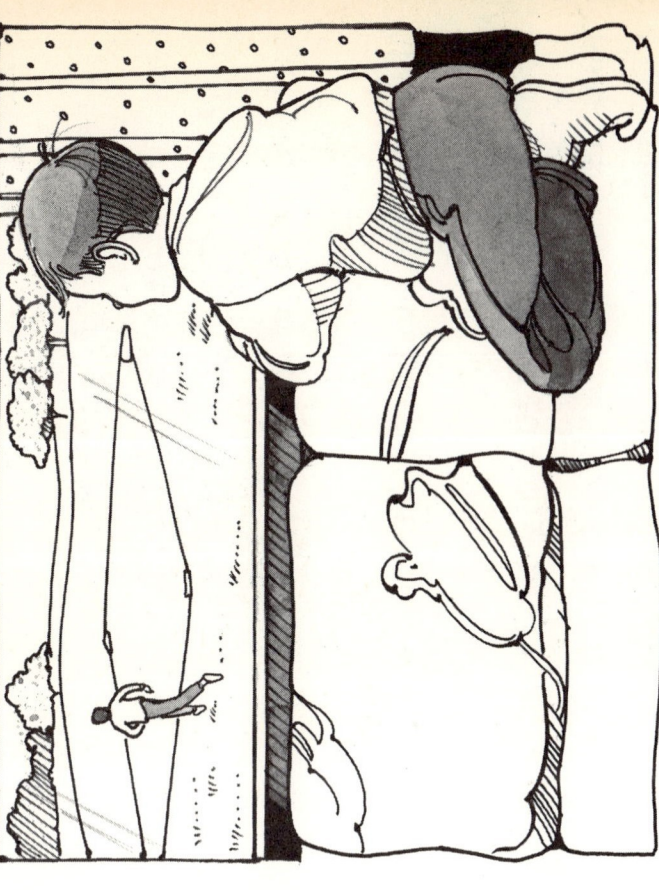

Sammy's father ran across the field. When he came back, he had Ann's bike and helmet.

Sammy and his dad went out to the bike path around the field. Sammy got on the bike. He was afraid at first, but his father held on so that Sammy wouldn't fall.

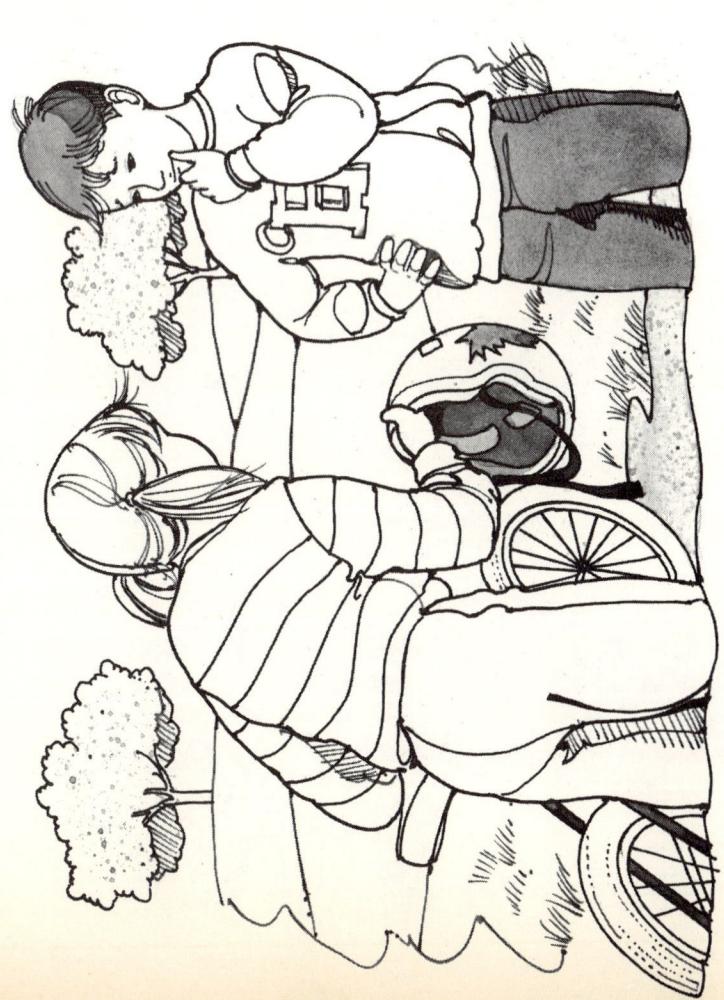

"Afraid of what?" asked Sammy.

"Are you afraid you will fall down?" asked Ann. "I heard someone say that you are afraid of everything."

"I am not afraid," said Sammy. "Anyway, I have to go. I think I just heard my dad calling me."

4 9

Then Sammy ran across the field to his house.

"Come back, Sammy!" yelled Ann. "You don't have to practice if you don't want to!"

But Sammy didn't hear Ann. He was at his front door in no time at all.

Sammy looked down. He was afraid he was going to cry.

"I know what we can do," said Dad. "You need practice, so I'll help you. I'll ask Ann if we can use her bike. Wait here. I'll be right back!"

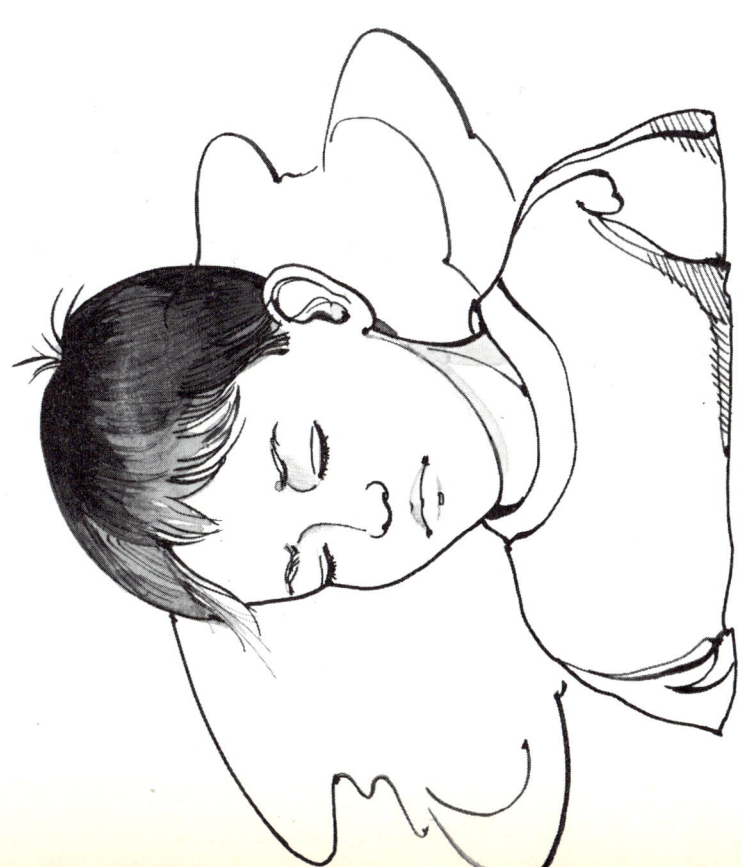

"Then did you ride?" asked Dad.

"No, I didn't." said Sammy. "Dad, I'm afraid. I wanted to practice riding the bike. But then I couldn't do it. Ann said she heard I was afraid of everything."

"Everyone is afraid sometimes," said Dad. "You aren't the only one."

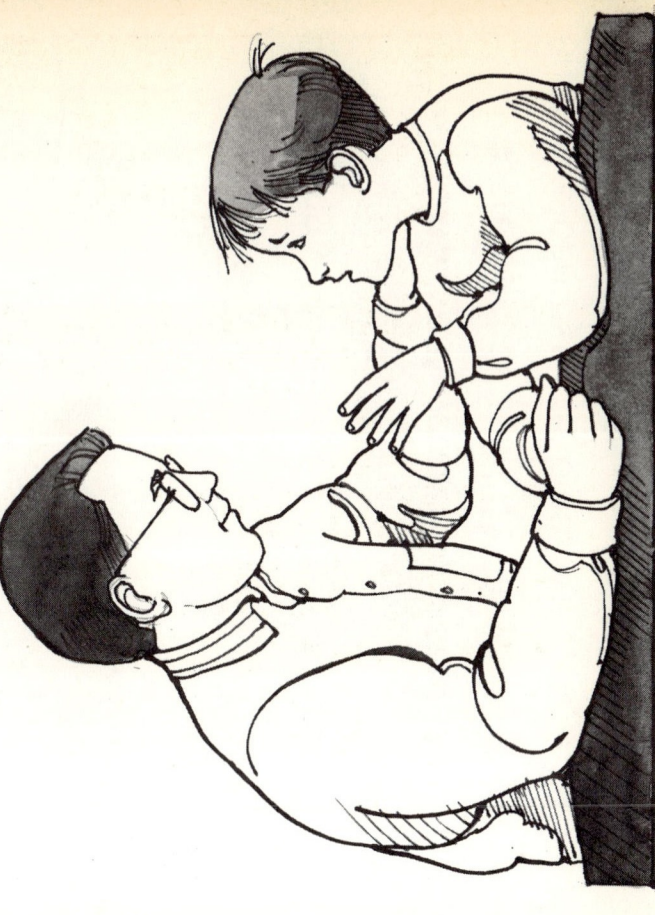

Sammy went inside his house and closed the door.

"Hi," said Sammy's dad. "Did you have fun? Did you ride Ann's bike?"

"I let her have the first turn," said Sammy. "She went all the way across the field."

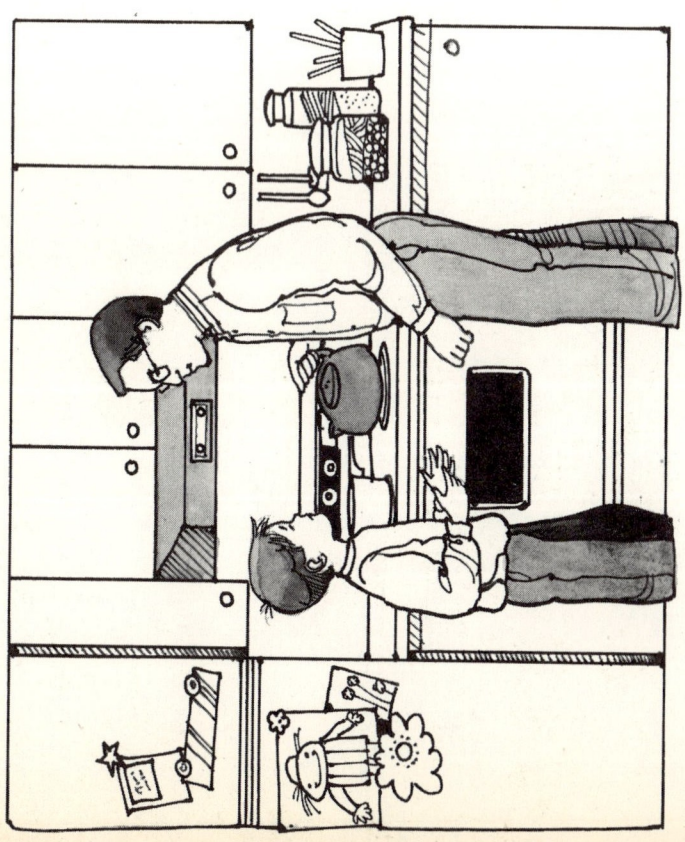

A VOICE IN THE TREES

by Stacy Kaufman

TAKE-HOME BOOK
SIDEWALKS SING
Use with "Matthew and Tilly."

© Harcourt Brace School Publishers

HARCOURT BRACE & COMPANY

Once upon a time, a bird named Birdie lived in an old oak tree along with many other birds. Birdie had a nice voice. Everyone loved his singing. Birdie always began to sing first thing in the morning.

When little birds grew up and moved away, one thing they always remembered was Birdie's wonderful voice.

1

So the bat moved to the old house. "Come and visit me once in a while," said Birdie with a happy voice. The bat smiled and waved a sleepy good-bye.

And that is just what happened. When Birdie was waking up, the bat remembered to visit him. But the bat never again heard Birdie's voice when he was trying to sleep.

12

Birdie thought for a while. Then he remembered something. "Come with me!" he shouted. "I know a place for you."

Birdie and the bat flew off to the old house that was not too far away. "Once, a long time ago, people lived in this house," said Birdie. "But they moved. You can live on the porch. My voice won't wake you anymore."

One morning, Birdie began singing just as he always did. His voice sounded wonderful. Then Birdie heard a high, screechy voice.

"You woke me up!" the voice said.

Birdie was sure the voice could not be talking to him. So Birdie began to sing another song.

"Stop that singing!" yelled the voice. "I told you once, and I don't want to say it again!"

3

Birdie began to think. He remembered things he knew about bats. He remembered that they *do* sleep in the daytime.

"Why don't you sleep in another place?" asked Birdie. "Then my voice wouldn't wake you up."

"You want me to move?" asked the bat. "I like this tree. I don't know another good place to live."

10

The bat looked at Birdie for a long time. Then he began to speak. "I didn't say that I didn't like your voice. It is a very nice voice. But bats are awake all night. We sleep in the daytime. Just when I began to sleep, you woke me up!"

Now Birdie began to feel afraid. Maybe the voice *was* talking to him. Birdie wanted to be brave, so he called out, "Is someone there?"

No one said anything. So Birdie began to sing another song. He made his voice a little louder this time. It made him feel strong and brave.

But Birdie didn't feel brave for very long, because the voice began to screech again.

"I told you once. I told you twice. Stop that singing! Now I'm coming over there."

Birdie was shaking. He wanted to feel brave, but he couldn't.

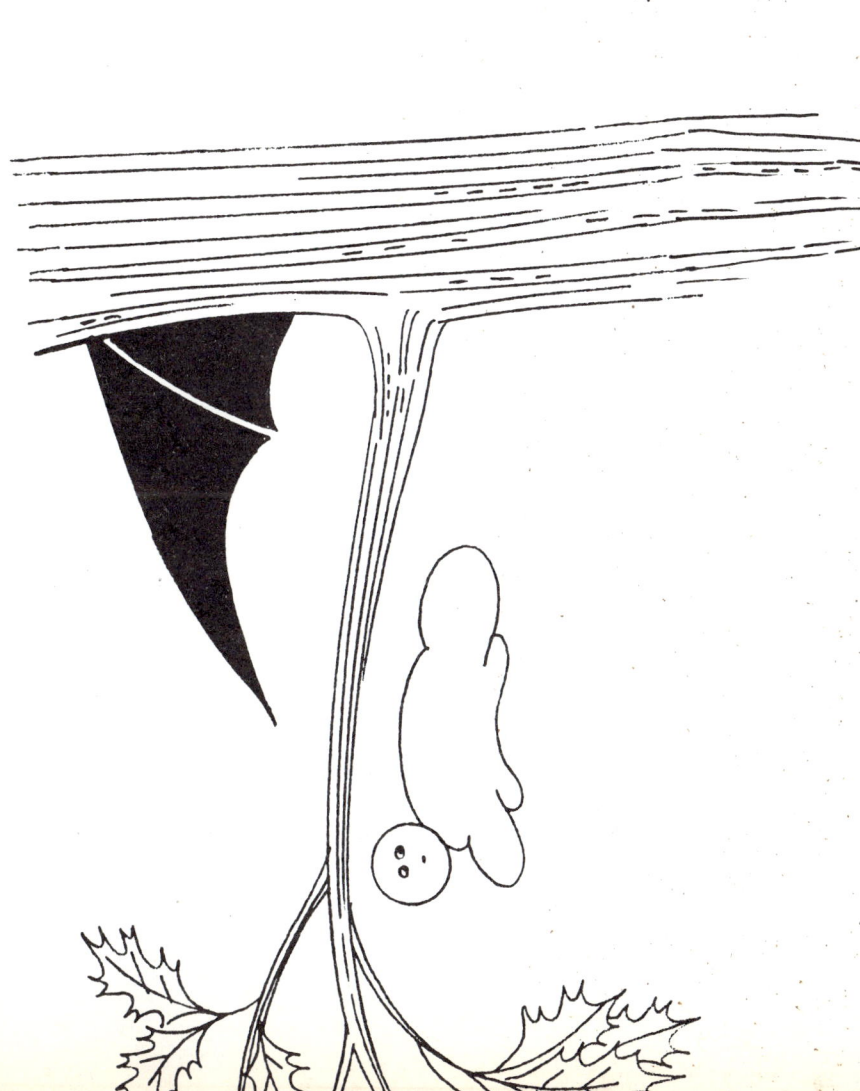

Birdie tried to sound brave, but his voice was shaking. "Everyone likes my voice," he said. "No one has ever talked to me like this before. Not once. Not ever. Why don't you like my singing?"

Then Birdie heard another sound. It sounded just like wings. Birdie began to feel better right away.

"It must be another bird," said Birdie. "I can get along with another bird."

But it wasn't a bird. It was a big bat!

"Hi," said Birdie in a tiny, little voice.

The bat didn't say "hi." He just started yelling. "I told you once. I told you twice. I told you not to sing. But you didn't stop!"

Nothing to Do

by Kim Noland

TAKE-HOME BOOK
SIDEWALKS SING
Use with "Arthur's Pet Business."

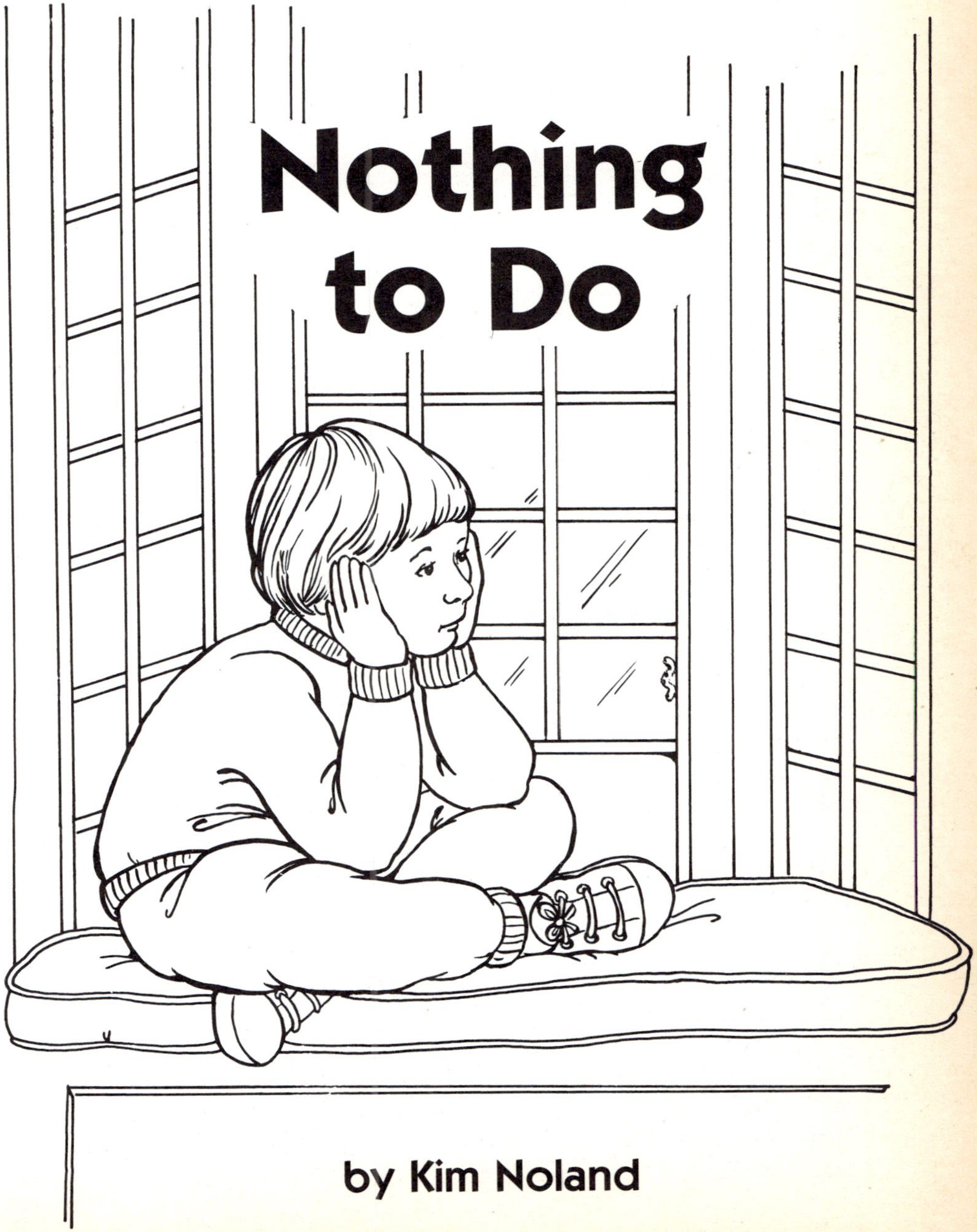

HARCOURT BRACE & COMPANY

It was Saturday, but Toby had nothing special to do. He wasn't allowed to go to the park by himself. He wasn't allowed to watch TV all day. He wasn't even allowed to talk on the phone for very long.

1

"Wake up," said Toby's mother.
"Was I dreaming?" asked Toby.
"Yes," said Toby's mother. "You're having a bad day, aren't you? Come on. Let's find something special to do together."

Toby smiled. "Thanks, Mom," he said. "But first I have some work to do."

Toby got up and cleaned his room, better than he ever had before. Then he was ready to do something special. He knew that he had earned it.

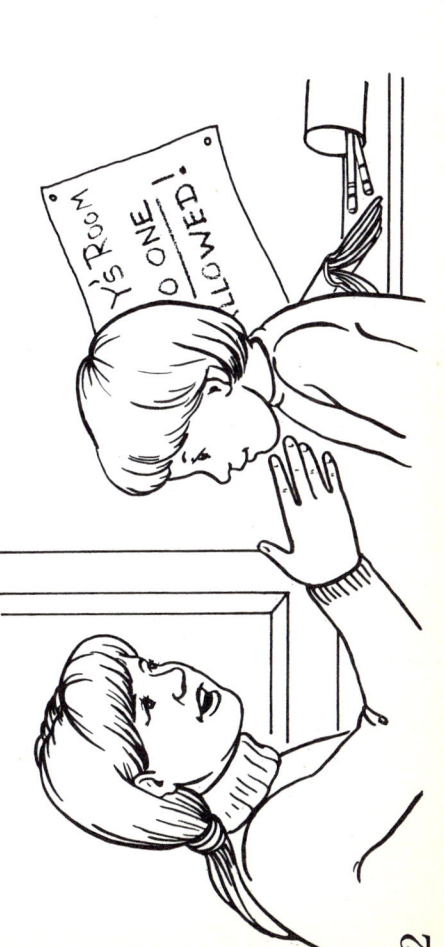

12

"I'm going to the phone!" said Toby. "I'm going to tell Mr. Samson what you did!"

But Toby couldn't get out of his room. The mess was too big. Milly laughed and laughed. Toby yelled and yelled.

11

Toby went into his room. He never took care of it. Toby's room was a mess. But he didn't seem to care.

2

Toby's mother came into his room.
"What are you doing, Toby?" she asked.
"Nothing," said Toby. "But I want to do *something*. I want to do something special. I'm so bored!"
"You could clean up your room," Toby's mother said. "It really is a mess. A little work wouldn't hurt you."
"That's not special," said Toby.

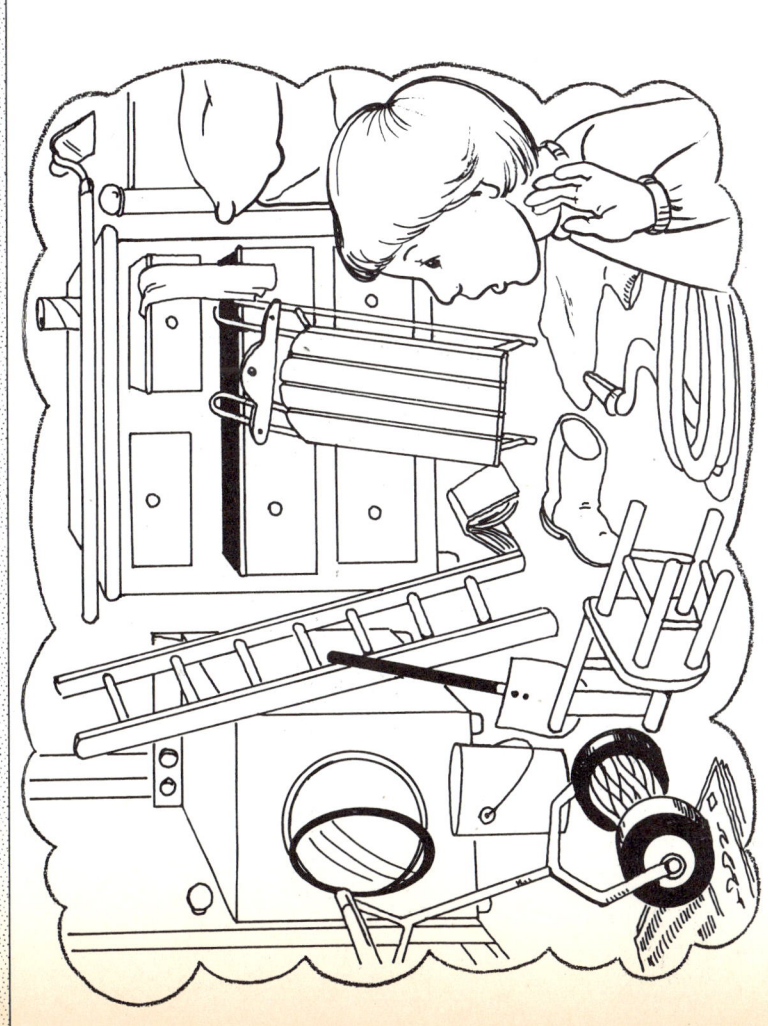

When Toby opened his eyes, he couldn't believe what he saw. "Where did this stuff come from?" yelled Toby. "Where's my money? I worked hard for it. I earned it. You're not allowed to keep it. I'll never find my money in this mess!"
"I don't care," said Milly.

Then Toby opened his piggy bank. Toby had earned most of his money by walking Mr. Samson's dog, Milly.

Toby's mother came back into the room. "Don't play with your money now," she said. "Please put it away. It's time to get to work."

"Keep your eyes closed," said Milly.

"Be careful with my money," said Toby. "I earned it doing work."

Toby closed his eyes and said, "One, two, three, ..." He could hear Milly leave his room and then come back many times. "... nine, ten, eleven, ..." Milly was doing a lot of work.

"I'm opening my eyes now!" said Toby.

"Well, okay," said Milly.

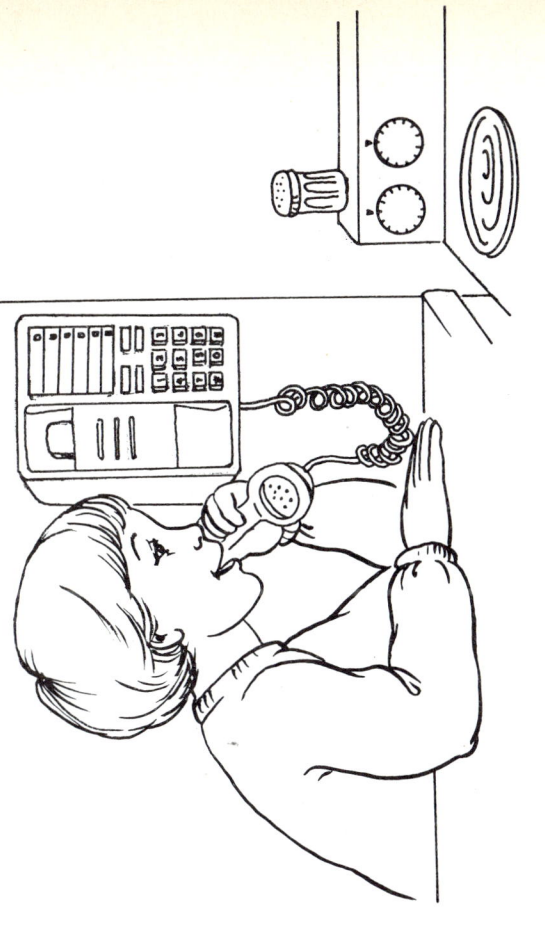

"Come on, Toby," said Milly. "Do you want to do something special?"

"Like what?" asked Toby.

"We could play hide-and-seek with your money," said Milly. "I will hide it and you can seek it. But if you can't find it, I get to keep it all. Don't worry. I'll just hide it in your room. Do you want to play?"

"Well, okay," said Toby.

Then Toby went to the phone to call his best friend, Max. "Come on over and help me clean my room!" said Toby.

"I can't," said Max. "I'm cleaning *my* room."

"Mom!" yelled Toby. "Can I go over to Max's house to help him clean his room?"

"No!" said Toby's mom. "You have your own mess to clean up!"

Toby hung up the phone and went back into his room. It began to rain, but Toby didn't care. He wasn't allowed to go anywhere. It wasn't going to be a special day after all. Toby began to clean up. But then he lay down on his bed. He fell fast asleep.

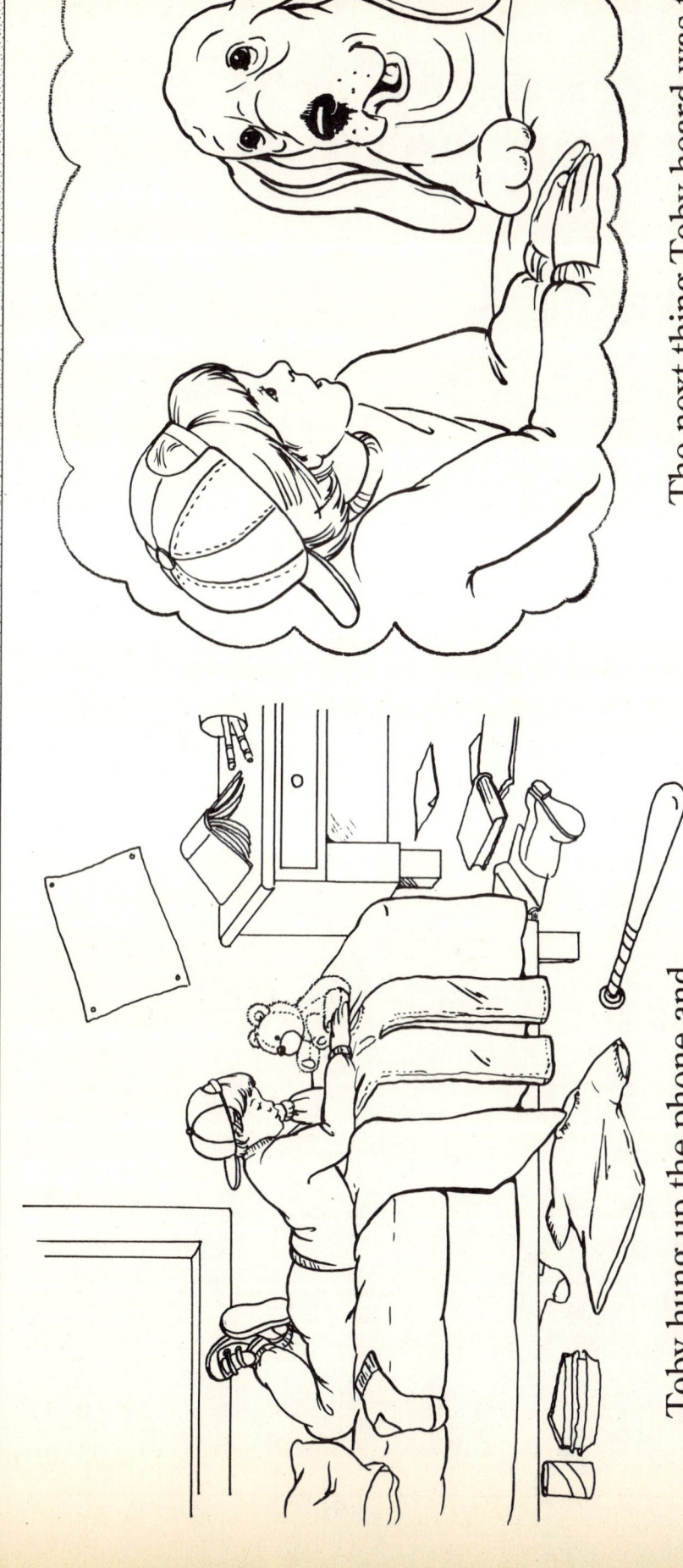

The next thing Toby heard was this: "Psst, psst! Toby! Wake up. I am here to play with you."

Toby looked at the floor. It was Mr. Samson's dog, Milly. And the dog was talking to Toby! "Now, *this* is special!" said Toby.

BEST FRIENDS

by Ellen Keller

TAKE-HOME BOOK
SIDEWALKS SING
Use with "I Have a Sister—My Sister Is Deaf."

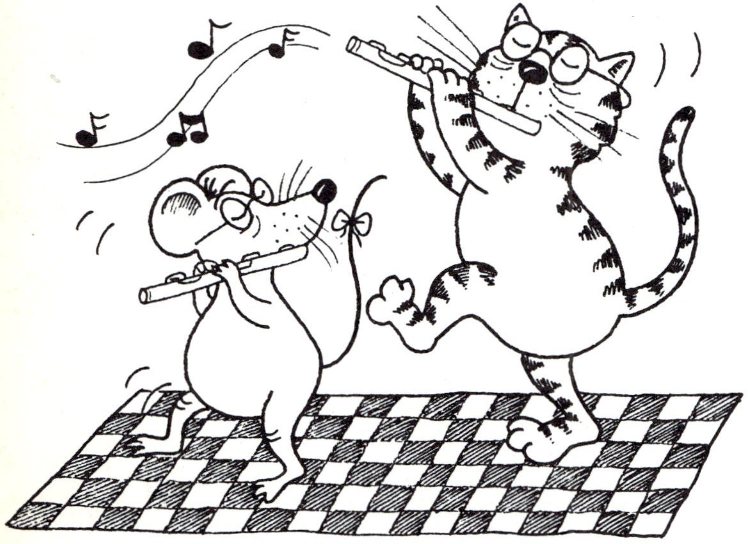

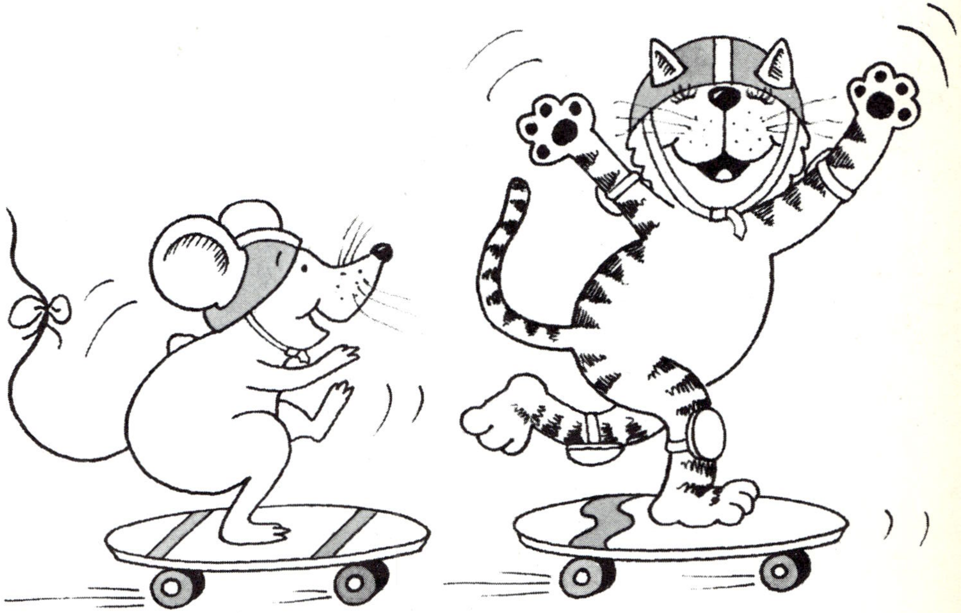

HARCOURT BRACE & COMPANY

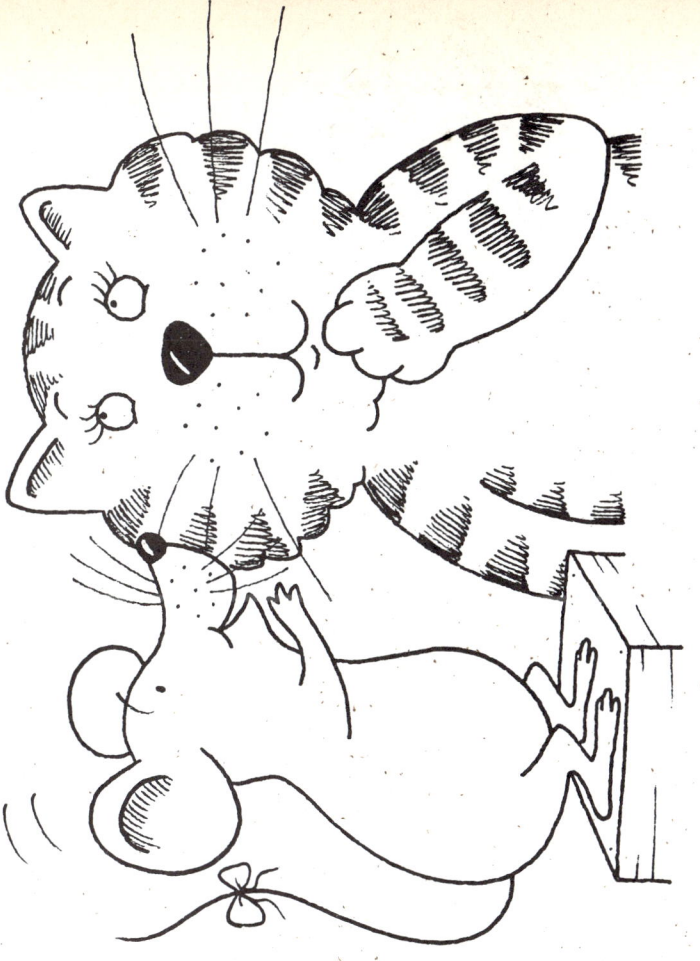

Cat and Mouse are best friends. No one understands it. Cat is kind and gentle. Mouse is kind and gentle, too. When Mouse talks, Cat listens. Cat understands Mouse. When Cat talks, Mouse listens. Mouse understands Cat. They like each other very much.

This story happened a long time ago. Cat and Mouse are grandmothers now. But they still see each other. When Mouse talks, Cat listens. They speak in gentle voices. When Cat talks, Mouse understands. They are still best friends.

Then all the cats began to talk at once. They had really bad feelings.

Then Mouse came back into the yard and cried, "Look, Cat! You left your flute across the street."

"Now I remember," said Cat. "Thank you for finding my flute, Mouse!"

The other cats were surprised. Some cats just walked away. Others stayed. "I learned something today," said one cat. "A cat *can* be friends with a mouse."

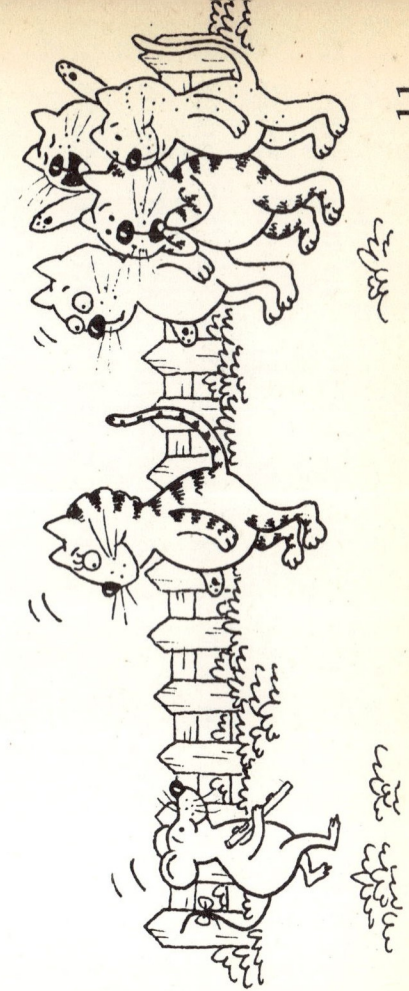

11

Cat has learned to play the flute. Mouse listens to her play. The music is sweet and gentle. It gives Mouse happy feelings.

"I will show you how to play," said Cat. "I learned, and so can you."

It took five days, but Mouse learned to play the flute.

One day Mouse was all alone in Cat's backyard. She saw the flute. She picked it up and began to play a sweet and gentle tune.

"She wouldn't do that," said Cat in a gentle voice. "She listens to me when I play my flute. She is my best friend."

Then the big cat spoke. "It's time you learned that a cat can't be friends with a mouse."

"That's not true," said Cat. "Mouse is a good friend. She understands me. She listens when I talk. I like to listen to her, too."

When Mouse had gone, all the cats came to Cat's yard. They all began to talk at once.

"We've learned something about your flute."

"We saw Mouse touching it."

"That made us mad."

"We think she took your flute."

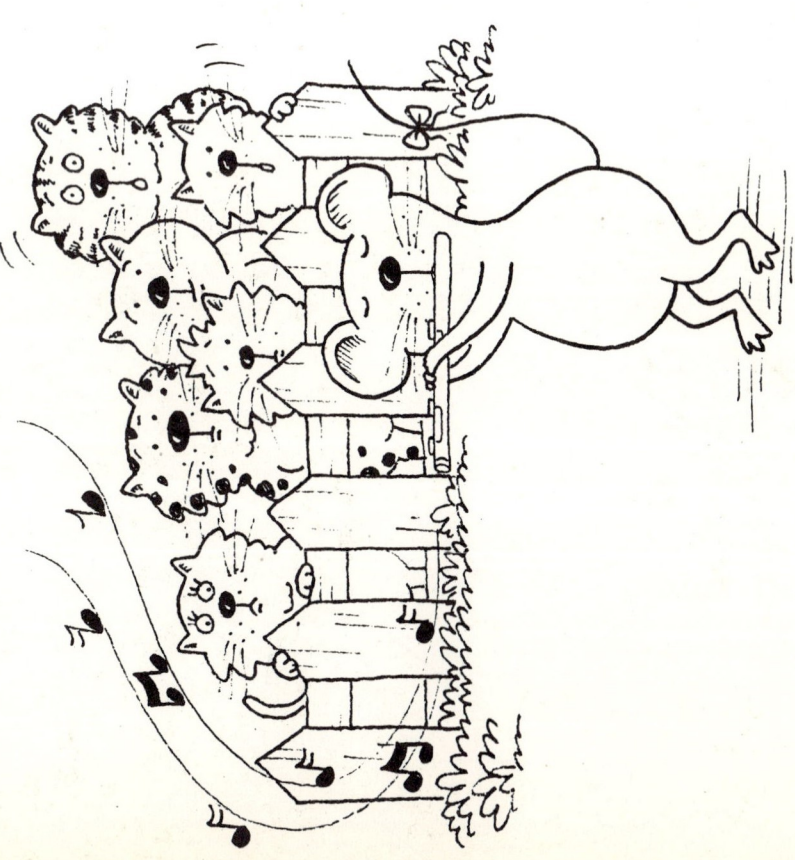

The other cats learned that Mouse was playing Cat's flute. They came running as fast as they could.

Then all the cats whispered at once.
"Look, she's playing Cat's flute."
"She shouldn't be touching Cat's flute."
"A *mouse* is playing Cat's flute."
"It gives me bad feelings."

The next day, Cat was in her yard. She looked upset.

"What's the matter?" Mouse asked in a gentle voice.

"My flute is missing," said Cat.

So Cat and Mouse looked for the flute. They looked all around, but they couldn't find the flute.

"You stay here," said Mouse. "I'll look across the street. Maybe the flute is over there."

Then all the cats whispered at once.

"I'll tell her. She listens to me."

"No, *I'll* tell her. I'll be gentle. I won't hurt her feelings."

"Listen," said the big cat. "We will *all* talk to her until she understands. It's time she learned what's right. We will come back later."

Then the biggest cat spoke. "A mouse should not be playing Cat's flute. Cat hasn't learned what we all know. A cat can never be friends with a mouse. We must tell Cat, but we will be gentle. We don't want to hurt her feelings."

PERFECT STEW

by Jeffrey Baxter

TAKE-HOME BOOK
SIDEWALKS SING
Use with "The Wolf's Chicken Stew."

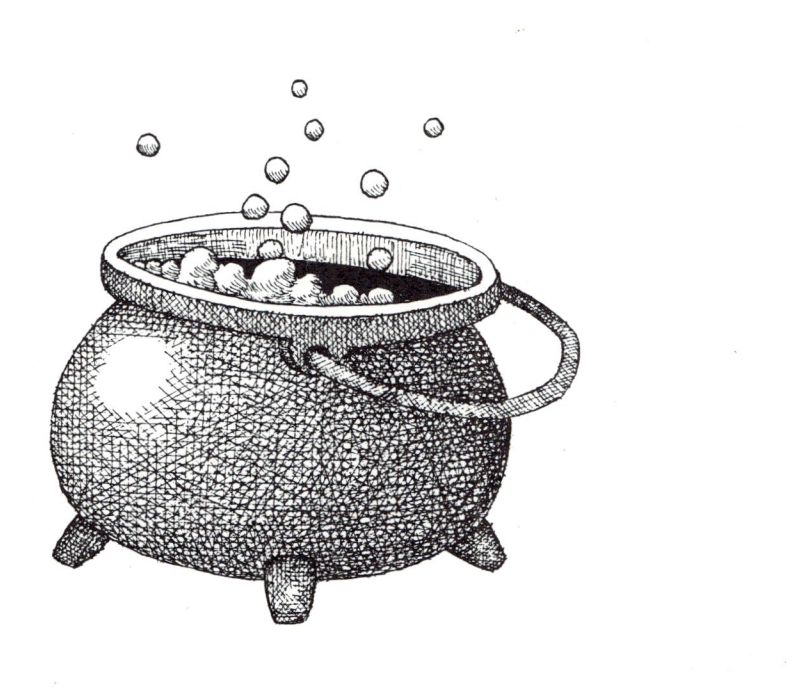

HARCOURT BRACE & COMPANY

Once a long, long time ago, a terrible troll moved into the forest. He unpacked his bags and started to cook right away.

"I will make some stew," said the troll. Then he put water in a big pot. He added salt and tasted the stew.

"Yum, it's delicious already," said the troll.

The animals went to the troll's home. The bear spoke up. "Hello, Mr. Troll. We have come to help you cook. We are friends, not your prey."

The animals began to cook. The stew turned out perfect and delicious. The troll ate it up. And so did all his new friends.

"I must search for something to add to the stew," said the troll. "The stew is delicious. But I can make it better."

So the troll stirred the stew, and as he stirred, he sang,

Delicious stew,
Perfect stew,
I will add my prey.
It will be a rabbit.
It will cook all day.

The animals began to feel sorry for him.

"He's eating salt and water," said one animal. "That won't make him strong. He needs plants to make that stew perfect. Should we tell him?"

The animals all said that they would help the troll. They went to find plants for the stew.

All the animals watched the troll.
They didn't know what to think. But
everybody knew this troll wasn't very
smart.

"That stew must taste terrible," said
a bird.

"He thinks it's perfect and delicious,"
said a rabbit.

"All that salt will be bad for him," said
a squirrel.

All the rabbits and other animals had
been listening.

"What's stew?" asked one rabbit.
"What's prey?" asked another rabbit.
"I don't know," said a third rabbit.
"But it can't be good. Let's go!"
And down the rabbit hole they went.

When the terrible troll went out to search for rabbits, he couldn't find any. So he went back home.

As the troll stirred his stew, he was thinking, "There are no rabbits. What else could I put in my stew?"

Then the troll got an idea. So as he stirred, he sang,

> Delicious stew,
> Perfect stew,
> I will add my prey.
> It will be a squirrel.
> It will cook all day.

The terrible troll made himself a big bowl of stew. He ate it right up. Then he began to sing,

> Delicious stew,
> Perfect stew,
> Dooby, dooby, hey!
> I can eat my stew like this
> Each and every day!

All the squirrels and other animals had been listening.

"Squirrel stew!" cried one squirrel. "What a terrible idea!"

"Terrible, just terrible!" said all the other squirrels.

"We will not be prey for the troll," said another squirrel. "Come on, let's go!"

And up the trees they went.

When the terrible troll went out to search for birds, he couldn't find any. So he went back home.

The troll stirred the stew. He tasted it and added more salt. "Delicious!" he cried. "Maybe I don't need any prey. The stew is perfect just as it is!"

When the troll went out to search for squirrels, he couldn't find any. So he went back home.

As the troll stirred his stew, he was thinking, "There are no squirrels. What else could I put in my stew?"

Then the troll got another idea. So as he stirred, he sang,

Delicious stew,
Perfect stew,
I will add my prey.
It will be a birdie.
It will cook all day.

All the birds and other animals had been listening.

"Eek!" screeched a crow. "I can't stand being called a birdie! I am a big, strong, perfect bird!"

"That's not the point," said a robin.

"Being perfect will land you in that stew!"

"Oops!" screeched the crow. "Let's get out of here!"

And he and the other birds flew off.

The Secret Friend

by Jeffrey Baxter

From Your Secret Friend

TAKE-HOME BOOK
SIDEWALKS SING
Use with "Everett Anderson's Friend."

HARCOURT BRACE & COMPANY

Emily is going to visit her grandma for the summer. Emily's family isn't going with her, so she is feeling sad. Grandma doesn't live too far away, but it seems like the other side of the world to Emily.

Emily won't know anyone besides Grandma. Nothing will be familiar to her. Emily realizes she will miss her family. She realizes she will miss her friends, too.

At last summer is over. Emily is going back to her family. "I'll miss you, Lauren," says Emily. "You're the best friend in the world."

"You're my best friend, too," says Lauren. "I'll write to you."

"I'll write back," says Emily.

When Emily gets home, everything looks familiar. She is glad to be back, but she misses Lauren. She writes to Lauren, and Lauren writes back. They both sign the letters "Your secret friend."

Now it is time to go. Emily's family says good-bye to her. "You will be good company for Grandma," says Emily's mom.

"Why can't Grandma come here?" asks Emily. "Then the whole family can be her company."

Emily wants to see Grandma, but she would rather stay home.

So Emily and Lauren play together all summer. Grandma has company and so does Emily. Emily goes everywhere with Lauren. Emily feels right at home.

A family friend is driving Emily to her grandma's house. Emily gets in the car. Then she sees some people coming. They are Emily's friends. They give Emily a book. "Thanks! I won't lose it," Emily says. Emily looks out at all the familiar faces. She feels sad to be leaving.

3

So Emily and her grandma go to visit Lauren and her family. Emily likes them very much. They are a lot like her own family.

"You are a smart girl," says Grandma to Lauren. "How in the world did you think of those notes?"

"I saw Emily," says Lauren. "I wanted to be her friend."

10

Emily waits some more, but no company comes. Then another note slides under the door. Emily opens the door fast. She sees her secret friend.

"Hi," says the girl. "I'm Lauren."
"Hi," says Emily. "I'm Emily. I like your notes. What's in this one?" Then Emily reads it.

To a secret friend and her grandma,
Come visit us at four.
We live by you, right next door.
From Lauren and her family

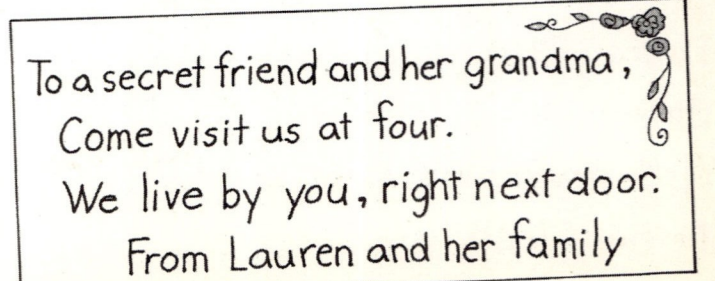

After a long drive, Emily gets to Grandma's house. "You are the best company in the world for me," says Grandma. Emily gives her a hug. Emily thinks that maybe this visit won't be so bad.
Emily tells Grandma all about her family. She knows that Grandma misses them, too.

After lunch, Grandma lies down to rest, so Emily goes out on the porch. She feels sad. She misses her family and friends. Emily wishes that she had some company.

She sees some kids across the street. "They could be my company," Emily thinks. The kids look at Emily. Then they go away. Other people go by, but no one looks familiar. Emily thinks she is the saddest girl in the whole world.

The next day, Emily finds another note under the door. Now the writing looks familiar. Emily realizes that it's from her secret friend. The note says,

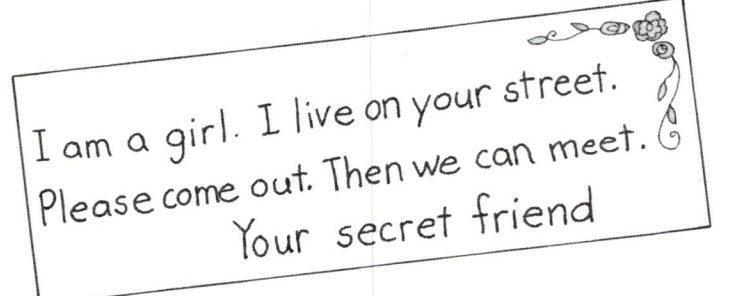

> I am a girl. I live on your street. Please come out. Then we can meet.
> Your secret friend

Emily looks out. No one is there. Emily puts the note away. She doesn't want to lose it.

After dinner, Emily looks at pictures of her family. She reads the book her friends gave her and then puts it in a safe place. She doesn't want to lose it.

Grandma realizes that Emily feels sad. "You will feel better when things are more familiar to you," says Grandma. "You'll see. You'll meet some friends."

Then Emily and Grandma hear something on the porch. They see a note sliding under the door. "What in the world is that?" asks Grandma.

Emily reads the note. It says,

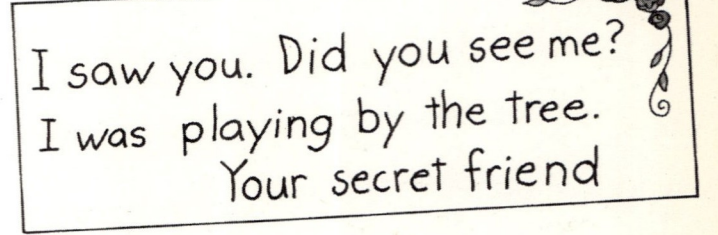

> I saw you. Did you see me?
> I was playing by the tree.
> Your secret friend

Emily realizes that the note is for her. She opens the door and looks out. No one is there, but Emily feels better right away. She thinks she will meet a friend.

TAKE-HOME BOOK
SIDEWALKS SING
Use with "Mitchell Is Moving."

The Gigantic Package

by Marilyn Wendt

HARCOURT BRACE & COMPANY

Wendell had a problem. He couldn't think of anything to give his mother for Mother's Day. He went through many stores, but he didn't get any ideas. He went through his house, but he didn't get any ideas. He went through all the closets. Then he got an idea.

"I will give my mother a package," said Wendell. "It will be a gigantic package!"

And Wendell came out of the gigantic package.

"Wendell! You're here!" said Mother. Everyone cheered, and then they helped Mother open her gifts. She didn't say so, but Wendell knew that she liked his gift best of all.

"Why are you looking in the closets?" asked Wendell's mother.

"I have a problem," said Wendell.

"What kind of problem?" asked his mother.

"A gigantic problem," Wendell answered.

"Can I help you?" asked Wendell's mother.

"I have to do this myself," answered Wendell.

"This is a problem," said Mother. "I can't have a happy Mother's Day without Wendell."

"We looked all through the house," said Mother. "Where can he be?"

"Here I am!" answered Wendell in a loud voice.

Then it was Mother's Day. The first thing in the morning, Mother and her family went into the living room. There was a pile of gifts for Mother and one big, gigantic package in the middle of them. But Wendell wasn't there.

"Where is Wendell?" Mother asked.

"We don't know," answered the brothers and sisters.

The whole family went through the house looking for Wendell, but they couldn't find him.

Wendell went downstairs. He liked thinking about his mother's package. He was having fun. Wendell looked through the whole basement until he found some boxes. First, he found a tiny one. "This would make a tiny package," said Wendell.

Then he found a gigantic box. "This will make a gigantic package," said Wendell. "This is just perfect!"

The next day, Wendell went through the house looking for his stickers. He found them and stuck them all over the box. The box was so big that Wendell used all of his stickers.

Wendell hid the package in the back corner of the basement. He didn't want his mother to see her gift.

Just then, all of Wendell's sisters and brothers came through the basement door.

"What are you doing?" they asked.
"Nothing," answered Wendell.
"What are you doing with that box?" they asked.
"It's a gift," answered Wendell.
"What will you put in it?" asked the brothers and sisters.
"I'm not putting anything in it," said Wendell. "The package *is* the gift."
All the brothers and sisters laughed.

Every day after that, Wendell went through the house looking for things for his package. One day, he found some paint. He painted the box red. His mother liked red best. The package was so large that it took Wendell most of the day to paint it.

"You have a problem," said one sister.

"You sure do," said a brother.

"Why?" asked Wendell.

"Because," answered the brother, "a package by itself is not a gift. There has to be something in it. I don't know what could have been going through your mind."

"I don't have a problem," said Wendell. "I have made up my mind. My present will be this gigantic package."

"Have it your way," answered the sisters and brothers as they went back out through the door.

Wendell thought about what his sisters and brothers had said. Then he got another good idea.

It's Not Fair!

by Jeffrey Baxter

TAKE-HOME BOOK
SIDEWALKS SING
Use with "Jamaica Tag-Along."

HARCOURT BRACE & COMPANY

Tim was good at making things. He never had to go to the store for toys. He already had things at home to make toys with.

Tim liked to use the old stuff his mom tossed out. Tim was busy making things all the time.

"It's not fair!" yelled Tim. Then he and his mom started to laugh.

"I already know what you're going to say," laughed Tim. "Tippy did it."

"Yes," said Mom. "Tippy likes to toss things around."

"Or maybe he can read," laughed Tim. "One of these boxes is a dog food box. I was so busy that I didn't feed him. I think Tippy is trying to tell me something!"

"Come on, Tippy," said Tim. "Let's eat!"

"Kenny is taking a nap," said Mom.

"It's not fair to blame him."

"Who did it then?" asked Tim.

"I don't know," said Mom. "Here, catch!" she said as she tossed Tim a small box. "Let's get busy. I'll help you repair the ramp."

In no time at all, Tim and his mom had repaired the car and the ramp.

All of a sudden, Tippy came running toward Tim. He bumped into the ramp and made a big mess!

One day, Tim was really busy. First, he had to repair one of his cars. When he had tossed the car into the toy box, a wheel had come off. The car wasn't hard to repair. He put the wheel back on. Then Tim rolled the car toward the wall. The car worked just fine.

Tim's cars and the ramp were all over the room. The wheels were off one car. "It's not fair!" he said to his mother.

"You can fix the car," said Tim's mom.

"But if you had put it away, it wouldn't have been broken."

"I already repaired that car once," said Tim. "It's not fair. Kenny is always playing with my things."

10

Tim wanted to race the car. So he made a ramp from old boxes his mom didn't want anymore.

Tim put the car he repaired at the top of the ramp with another car. He rolled them both down the ramp toward the wall. The car he had repaired won the race!

Tim was so busy playing that he didn't feed his dog, Tippy. Tim's mother had already told him two times to do it.

3

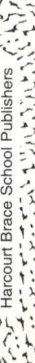

"Feed Tippy," called Tim's mom. "Or did you do it already?"

"No, I didn't," said Tim. "Can I feed him later? I'm too busy to feed him now."

"Busy," said Tim's little brother, Kenny. He never said more than one word at a time.

Kenny tossed his ball toward Tim's ramp. Tim stopped it just in time.

When Tim got home, his mother said, "You never bothered to put away your toys, Tim. Do you think that's fair to the rest of us?"

"No," said Tim. "It's not fair. From now on I'll remember to clean up."

So Tim went in to put away his things. But what he saw really bothered him. "It's not fair," he said to his mother. "Look what Kenny did!"

4

"Stop, Kenny," said Tim. "You tossed that ball toward my ramp. If you break it, I'll have to repair it. So stop!"

"Stop!" laughed Kenny.

Then Tim laughed, too. His brother was little, but he could already say some words. Tim liked his brother. But Tim didn't like it when Kenny bothered him.

"Tim," called his mother. "I already told you. Feed the dog!"

Tim and his friends watched a man repair his bike. Then they tossed a ball to each other. Tim forgot to watch the time. He was just too busy.

Then one of Tim's friends said it was time for dinner. So they all ran off toward home.

Tim knew his mother was busy. She had already fed Tippy once today because Tim didn't do it. Tim knew that wasn't fair because Tippy was his dog.

Tim got some dog food and the dish. Then he called, "Come on, Tippy!" Tippy came running toward Tim.

When they got outside, Tim saw his friends coming toward him. "Let's go to the park!" they called.

"Mom, I'm going to the park!" Tim called.

Tim forgot all about Tippy. He never fed him. He just left with his friends.

After Tim got to the park, he remembered that he hadn't fed Tippy. It bothered him. But he was already at the park, and he didn't want to go back home.

Mallard's Adventure

by Ellen Keller

TAKE-HOME BOOK
SIDEWALKS SING
Use with "Abuela."

HARCOURT BRACE & COMPANY

Mallard was a little duck. He swam on a beautiful lake with lots of other ducks. Every day, Mallard watched the big ducks as they soared high above the lake.

"I want to fly high, too," said Mallard to his mother. "I want to have an adventure."

1

Time passed, and Mallard grew big and strong. The trees on the lake turned to beautiful red, yellow, and orange.

One day, all the ducks soared high above the lake. Then they flew away. They would fly to a country where it is warm for the winter. Mallard was having his adventure at last!

12

It was Mallard's mother. She flew down next to Mallard. She put her wings around him. He felt warm and safe.

"I just wanted to have an adventure," said Mallard. "I wanted to fly to another country."

"I know," said Mallard's mother. "And we will go someday—together."

"You're too little to fly high above the lake," said Mallard's mother. "When you're big, you will go places. We'll fly together to another country. We'll fly above busy cities and have a great adventure."

"Can't we go now?" asked Mallard. "I want to see something beautiful. I am big. I can have an adventure now."

"No," said Mallard's mother. "You must get bigger. Then we can fly together."

Mallard's mother flew off with the other ducks. Mallard watched her as she soared quickly over the water.

"This is not a good adventure," Mallard said. "I thought it would be beautiful. I thought I would see cities and go to another country. But I'm too cold and wet now."

Mallard waited. He wanted to go home, but he realized he didn't know which way to go. Mallard was lost.

Then Mallard heard something high above his head. Someone was calling him. The call made Mallard happy.

Mallard watched his mother fly up so high above the lake that he couldn't see her anymore. "I want to have an adventure now," said Mallard.

So Mallard swam to the other side of the lake. None of the other ducks could see him. Mallard flew up high. He soared into the sky above and then back to the lake.

Mallard turned around and flew toward home. As he flew, the sky became dark.

Then the rain and wind came. Mallard was getting very tired, but he kept on going. Mallard looked down. The land below didn't look so beautiful to him now. Mallard stopped to rest in some tall weeds.

Mallard landed in the bushes. Then he rested.

"That was easy," said Mallard. "I can do it. I'm big enough to see busy cities. I want to see a beautiful country. I'm going now!"

Mallard liked flying high above the trees. He flew over the hills. Mallard flew for a long time.

Then Mallard saw a big city. It was far away. Mallard was getting tired. It was hard for him to stay high above the trees.

"I'd better go home," said Mallard.

"Today I had an adventure. I can have an adventure in the city some other day."

Mallard took off into the sky. But this time, he kept on going.

"What would the other ducks say if they could see me?" Mallard was thinking. "They might say that I am big. They might say that I'm going to have an adventure. They might even say that I look beautiful!"

Mallard looked at the land and water below.

"It looks so beautiful from here," said Mallard. "I am having an adventure!"

The Twin Detectives

by Stacy Kaufman

TAKE-HOME BOOK
SIDEWALKS SING
Use with "Six-Dinner Sid."

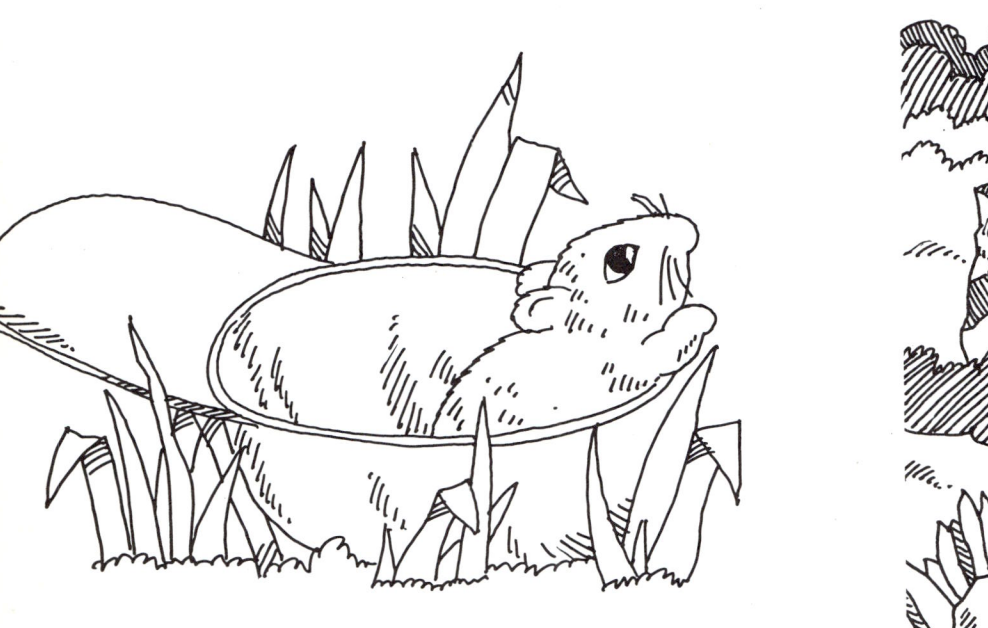

Harcourt Brace School Publishers

HARCOURT BRACE & COMPANY

Mindy and Mandy were twins, but they were as different as night and day. They looked different. They acted different. But they were best friends.

"I'm glad you came back," said Mr. Jones. "That hamster you caught is mine. When I discovered he was gone, I was so sad. But when I saw you holding Hammy so gently, I could tell that you really liked him. So I thought it would be okay if you kept him. Hamsters are for kids anyway."

"No, they're not," said Mandy. "Besides, I think he misses you, too!"

So Mr. Jones got his hamster back. And he told the girls to come back any time to visit Hammy.

Mindy and Mandy were alike in one way. They were both detectives. They discovered clues. They found and caught runaway pets and brought them back to their owners.

Mindy and Mandy lived with their mother and father, Grandma, and Uncle Jim in a big old house. It was a great place for detectives to live.

"I saw a bag of dog food on his porch," said Mandy. "As long as Mr. Jones has lived there, he's never had a dog."

"Hamsters eat dry dog food sometimes," said Mindy.

So they all went to see Mr. Jones again.

One day, Mindy and Mandy wanted to do something different. They went through a hole in the fence to the yard next door. Long ago, the girls had discovered the hole in the fence. The owners had always let Mindy and Mandy play in their yard.

That night, the whole family talked about what to do.

"I caught the hamster, so I should keep him," said Mandy. "But its owners might be sad because they miss their pet."

"Maybe the owners lived here before, but now they have moved away," said Mindy.

"I thought Mr. Jones was acting odd when we told him we caught a hamster," said Mindy.

Mindy and Mandy went to their favorite place under the trees. "Let's be detectives today," said Mindy.

"But we were going to do something different," said Mandy. "That's not different."

"Shhh," whispered Mindy. "I hear something. It's something really different. It's not birds singing. It's not the wind blowing. It sounds different, like something digging."

"We've caught a hamster," the girls said. "We're looking for the owners. Do you know where this hamster might have lived before it got lost?"

But no matter how hard they tried, Mindy and Mandy didn't find the owners.

Mandy jumped behind Mindy. "I hear something digging, too—digging with big paws," she whispered. "I think it might be a lion who ran away from its owners at the zoo. Or maybe it's something else . . . ."

"Stop kidding around, Mandy," whispered Mindy. "It could be just an animal that lives here in the bushes."

That night the detectives, Mindy and Mandy, spoke to all the pet owners who lived on the street. Uncle Jim went with them.

"You caught a hamster!" said Mindy.

"I wonder who the owners are," said Mandy. "I thought I had seen all the pets that live on this street."

"We have to find the owners," said Mindy. "This will be a good job for detectives. We can call it 'The Case of the Missing Owners.'"

Mindy and Mandy looked in the bushes. They each went a different way around the bushes. They met back where they had started. They had not seen anything.

Mindy turned to go. Then Mandy put her cap down over something under a bush. "I caught something!" she said.

"Oh, you did not!" said Mindy. "You're just kidding again."

"I caught something," Mandy whispered again. "Look!"

Disgrace in Dog Town

by Marilyn Wendt

TAKE-HOME BOOK
SIDEWALKS SING
Use with "Old Henry."

Harcourt Brace School Publishers

HARCOURT BRACE & COMPANY

Dog Town is a fine place. All the grown-up dogs are ladies and gentlemen. All the puppies have good manners. Nothing bad ever happens in Dog Town. Life is slow and quiet. Dog Town is perfect. Well, at least that's the way it was until the great disgrace!

Dazzle Dog left Dog Town. Now he moves from town to town. He still has plans for the Dog Circus. But he has decided that he wants to find a town where there is a lot of fooling around and barking. He wants to find a town where no one has ever heard of the word "disgrace."

One day Dazzle Dog decided to move to Dog Town. Dazzle Dog called all the ladies and gentlemen to a meeting.

"I have big plans to start a circus," he said. "I have decided that your children can be in it. They can learn to do tricks. Any puppy who moves fast and jumps high will be a star in the Dazzle Dog Circus!"

The ladies and gentlemen put signs up all over town. "Be a star in school" said one sign.

The puppies helped each other read the signs. They talked about all the things they had done in school. One by one, they made plans to go back. They decided that nothing would stop them.

"This is a disgrace!" said one of the ladies. "I don't want my children in your circus. We will have nothing to do with your plans!"

Other dogs didn't know what to think. They wanted to wait before they decided.

3

Then one of the ladies spoke up.

"We have to make some plans," she said. "We have to do something about this. I have decided that we must get our children back to school. Who will help me with my plans?"

All the ladies and gentlemen decided to think of a good plan together.

10

Most of the puppies didn't think it was a disgrace at all. They wanted nothing more than to be the stars of the circus. So they decided to practice some tricks. They got so excited that some of them even barked.

"Barking is bad manners," said one of the ladies.

"Yes, it is," said one of the gentlemen. "I haven't decided about the circus yet, but I know I don't like barking."

"What a disgrace," said a gentleman. "I had such plans for my children! And now my son does nothing but circus tricks. When one of my daughter's friends does a trick, my daughter does it, too. It's terrible."

"It *is* a disgrace!" all the dogs said, turning to each other. "There has never been such a problem in Dog Town!"

Every puppy wanted to be the star of the circus. So all of them worked harder on their tricks. It snowed, but they decided to practice anyway. It rained, and they *still* practiced. Nothing could keep the puppies from doing their tricks.

One of the ladies decided to have a meeting of all the dogs in Dog Town.

"It's a disgrace!" she said. "Our puppies will grow up, but they will not be good readers or writers. They have no plans to go to school."

Another one of the ladies was so upset that she almost started barking.

"We've got to do something," she said. "My child runs from place to place. She moves so fast that I don't get to see her."

Then the puppies said they didn't have time to go to school. They decided it would be better to be stars in the circus. Before long, the puppies almost forgot how to read and write.

Now the puppies did nothing but practice, practice, practice. They didn't make a move unless it was to do a trick. Each puppy wanted to be a circus star.

The Dog Town grown-ups decided that this was not good. The ladies and gentlemen had had enough of Dazzle Dog's circus.

Robot Camp

by Kim Noland

TAKE-HOME BOOK
SIDEWALKS SING
Use with "Little Penguin's Tale."

HARCOURT BRACE & COMPANY

One time, I went to a robot camp.
Everyone there was a robot, except for me.
Here's what happened.

I couldn't wait to go to Robot Camp!
I gathered all my camp clothes together.
And quick as a wink, I was packed and ready to go.

The robots had found some boy food. They had peas with milk on them. They had gathered bread, berries, and peanut butter and made a sandwich.

Most of the time, I eat everything, except peas. But now I ate *all* the food. It wasn't bad.

The robots were so happy that they wanted to dance. So I played some silly tunes and joined in the dancing. Robot Camp was going to be great!

My dad drove me to camp and said good-bye to me at the gate. Some robots gathered around me. They seemed happy to see me there.

The robots were all the same size, except for one who was bigger. He spoke to me, half in people talk and half in robot talk. He said, "U-R-2-COME-WITH-US."

Then all the robots walked in a line out of the lunchroom. They didn't even see that I hadn't joined them.

I felt bad. I shouldn't have said anything about the food.

I gathered up everything and put it in the trash can, except for the bowls and the tray. Then I didn't know what else to do, so I sat down and played a few tunes on my harmonica.

After a while, the robots came back. All the robots gathered around me. "LOOK-WHAT-WE-HAVE-4-U," said B-4.

All the robots gathered around me. Then they made a line. I joined the line, and we walked to the big house.

Inside the house, the big robot showed me where I would sleep. "U-WILL-SLEEP-IN-MY-ROOM," he said. "R-U-OK-IN-THE-TOP-BUNK?"

"Sure," I said.

B-4 was quick to see what was wrong. "I-C-U-CAN'T-EAT-ROBOT-FOOD," he said. "U-R-A-BOY. U-NEED-BOY-FOOD."

Then all the robots gathered in a group. B-4 joined them. They made quick beeping and talking sounds. It almost seemed as if they were singing robot tunes.

I started unpacking my bags, and the big robot joined in. He gathered up my socks and put them in the trash can. I got them back fast. I found out that robots think nothing is good except things that are hard. I showed the robot my writing paper. He did not understand how it was used. He thought it was something to eat. I was quick to take it back.

Then I found my harmonica and started playing some tunes. The robot started making quick, jerky moves. He said he was dancing, so I joined in.

I got my food and so did B-4. We went to a long table. The other robots joined us. I looked at the food.

In one bowl there was nothing except cut-up paper salad. In another bowl, there was nothing except nails and little bolts. The robots called it stew. I began to think that I was going to be very hungry at camp.

The robot told me he was having fun. I asked him what his name was. He said his name was B-4. He said he had that name because he was the biggest and because he could do everything B-4 all the others could, except me.

When we got to the lunchroom, everyone gathered around to see what was for lunch. Everyone was quick to get in line—except me. I was upset. Robot food was not the kind of food I was used to eating. But I didn't know what else to do, so I joined the line.

Then other robots gathered at our door. They had come to get us for lunch. They also wanted to see my things.

B-4 was quick to show them my socks. They all laughed, and I joined in. Then one robot gathered up my baseball cards. He thought they were food. I played some tunes on my harmonica so that he would put the cards down and dance.

I was having a lot of fun, except for one thing. I was hungry. So I spoke in robot, "R-U-HUNGRY-4-LUNCH?"

The robots thanked me for remembering lunch, and off we went.

I played some more tunes on my harmonica as we walked to the lunchroom. B-4 began to dance. All the other robots joined in. Everyone was dancing, except me. Then I joined in the dancing. The robots thought my dancing was funny. They all laughed, and I joined them in that, too.

New Friends Festival

by Kim Noland

New Friends Festival

TAKE-HOME BOOK
SIDEWALKS SING
Use with "Fiesta!"

HARCOURT BRACE & COMPANY

Harcourt Brace School Publishers

Something important was happening in second grade. The class was getting three new children from a school that had just closed.

Even before the new kids came, everyone felt happy.

"Let's celebrate," everyone said. "We are getting new friends."

Then the new girl, Amanda, went to the front of the room. "We like your New Friends Festival," she said. "You made us feel important. So we want to sing a song for you."

Here's the song they sang.

You are all so very cool.
And we really like your school.
You are friendly, nice, and kind.
Better friends we'll never find!

And everyone clapped and cheered.

"Yes, let's celebrate," said Rodney. "We can even have a party when they come."

"That will make them feel important," said Molly. "They might even forget to miss their old school."

"I know," said Juan. "We can call it the 'New Friends Festival.'"

Before the end of the day, the new kids met together in a corner. They were talking to each other.

"I wonder what's wrong," said Rodney.

"Maybe they don't like our New Friends Festival," said Beany.

Everyone felt sad.

"That would be nice," said Mrs. Jackson. "The new children would feel very welcome if we had a festival for them. That would be a good way to celebrate making new friends."

"Let's celebrate!" everyone called out.

In the afternoon, the class had their party. Beany told the new kids about the New Friends Festival.

"You are important to us," she said. "We want to be your friends."

Then the class sang their song. They taught the song to the new kids.

After singing, they ate the food they had made. Everyone was having fun.

First, the class had reading and then math. Everyone told the new kids what the class had been taught so far. Then, the new kids told about the math *they* had been taught and the stories *they* had read. They even showed books that they had brought along.

Then everyone began to work on the New Friends Festival. Some girls and boys made signs. The signs said, "Welcome new friends! You are important! We like you!"

Then everyone cleaned up the room. Everyone had a job. Everyone felt important.

The next morning, everyone got to school on time. It was going to be a busy day. It was time to celebrate the New Friends Festival.

The first thing in the morning, Mr. Chang brought in the new children. Everyone said, "Hello."

Then Mrs. Jackson showed the new kids where to sit. They seemed to feel at home right away.

"We should sing a song to our new friends when we have the party," said Rodney.

"We could even make one up," said Tracy. "We could call it the 'New Friends Song.' We can make up new words to 'Twinkle, Twinkle, Little Star.'"

We are happy you are here.
Hope your day is filled with cheer.
You're important to us all,
Summer, winter, spring, and fall.
Help us as we celebrate.
You're our friends, and you are great!

Beany was the class president. She had something important to say.

"Tomorrow is the big day. What can we do to make the new kids feel happy?"

"I know," said Thomas. "We can have a buddy sit with each new friend to be a helper."

Then Kelly spoke. "We can play with the new kids and sit with them at lunch time."

Other children had good ideas, too.

The next day, the class went shopping. They were buying things for the New Friends Festival party.

Tracy had made a list. She didn't want to forget anything important. She even crossed each food off the list as soon as another child put that food in the shopping cart.

TAKE-HOME BOOK
SIDEWALKS SING
Use with "Miss Eva and the Red Balloon."

FAVORITE THINGS

by Ellen Keller

HARCOURT BRACE & COMPANY

Harcourt Brace School Publishers

Danny looked through his window. New people were moving in next door. Big men hurried back and forth carrying boxes and chairs.

Danny looked at everything. He tried to tell if the people had any children. Then a man brought a bike out of the truck. "This family must have children," said Danny.

Danny hurried away.

"Wait!" Carlos called out.

Danny turned around. Carlos wasn't crying at all. He was laughing! "I don't want to break your favorite things," he said. "Let's just start all over. Let's act like we are just meeting now."

"Okay!" said Danny. And the boys hurried off to the park to play their second-favorite game—baseball.

Danny saw a boy come out of the house. He had Danny's favorite game under his arm.

"I'm going to go over and talk to that boy," said Danny. "Maybe he wants to play with me."

Danny walked over to Carlos's house. When Carlos saw Danny, he quickly hid the book he was reading. It was his favorite. He didn't want anything to happen to it.

"Hi," said Danny. "You can keep my checkerboard if you want to. I'm sorry that I put that big, round spot on yours."

Carlos didn't say anything.

Then Danny tried to be funny. "So, do you want to come over and rip up my favorite mask?"

Carlos covered up his face and began shaking. Danny felt terrible. He thought Carlos was crying.

Danny hurried over to the house next door. "Hi," he said. "My name is Danny. That's my favorite game!"

"Hi, I'm Carlos," said the boy. "Checkers is my favorite game, too."

3

Danny didn't see Carlos for two days. He felt bad. He brought out all his toys and tried to play. But he really didn't feel like it. Sometimes making new friends was hard.

Danny's dad had told him that he should say "I'm sorry" when things go wrong. Danny had tried that before, and it had helped. Maybe he would try saying "I'm sorry" now.

10

"Do you want to come over and play checkers?" asked Danny.

"I have to ask my mom," said Carlos. He hurried into his new house, and he came right back out again.

"That's my favorite mask," yelled Carlos. "You ripped it!"

Danny yelled back, "I never tried to rip your mask. I'm going home!"

The next day, Danny was thinking about how he had yelled at Carlos. He felt bad about it.

Danny went over to Carlos's house. He brought his favorite mask along. It was an ape mask with round, red eyes.

Carlos had a favorite mask, too. It was a monster mask with round, scary eyes. He brought it out and put it on.

At first the boys played and laughed at each other's faces. Then Danny tried to grab Carlos's mask. Carlos pulled away, and the mask ripped.

The boys hurried over to Danny's house. Carlos took his checkers game with him.

"Do you want some milk?" asked Danny. "It's my favorite drink."

"Sure," said Carlos. "It's my favorite, too."

Danny poured the milk. Then the boys sat down to play.

Carlos opened the box and began to take out some checkers. "I would like to have the red checkers," he said. "Red is my favorite."

Red was Danny's favorite, too. When Danny tried to grab the red checkers, he bumped the checkerboard. Carlos's milk fell over onto the checkerboard.

"Look what you made me do!" yelled Danny.

Danny brought a rag and tried to wipe up the board. It was too late. There was a big, round spot in the middle of Carlos's checkerboard.

Carlos picked up his game, looked at Danny, and hurried home.